FAITH, FREEDOM & POLITICS

David Tipton

DEDICATION

To the District Board of
The Mississippi District
United Pentecostal Church

As patriotic Americans I believe the flag should wave high, yet the cross must stand higher.

Table of Contents

ACKNOWLEDGEMENTS

My name is on the front of this book as the author, and that is somewhat misleading. As with any project, there is no such thing as a one-man orchestra. Many talented individuals using their skills produce the beautiful sounds of a symphony.

My heartfelt thanks go out to:

My wife, Gwen, who remains tenaciously committed to me, our children and grandchildren. I am a blessed man.

My executive secretary, Kristina Osborne devoted many hours making all the pieces work. You are a God-send.

The Mississippi District Political Liaison and my executive assistant, Ron Matis has shared my dream for several years in building strong relationships with our elected officials. He has worked tirelessly increasing the footprint of the Mississippi District which reaches from our State Capital all the way to the United States Capitol. Every district needs a Ron Matis!

A comedian said he was once mugged. He was beaten up, his face blackened and bruised. Someone asked him, "Why didn't you fight back?" His answer was, "I started to, but decided not to get involved."

The Bible teaches us to do everything possible to be good citizens and to be involved for the betterment of our society. In Jeremiah 29:7 (NIV) God tells us to "seek the peace and prosperity of the city to which I have carried you... because if it prospers, you too will prosper."

It is time to get involved!

PREFACE

Exercising our Christian citizenship is crucial in today's world. If we want to make our witness, knowledge, and influence count,

There are specific and effective ways to do this. The Mississippi District has developed a model and valuable information in this particular area. These recommendations are both practical and in alignment with the Apostolic beliefs and values.

This booklet serves as a much-needed guide to our Districts, Pastors, Churches and even to individual Christians as they play a part in daily civic life.

I sincerely hope each District of the United Pentecostal Church International and other Apostolic Movements will use these strategies to raise up beneficial, resourceful Christian citizenship to improve our communities, states, and our world. The dedicated men and women of the Church have a glorious opportunity in this day and time to employ Christian values and models to the political structure.

David Tipton

Chapter One

ALL CHRISTIANS ARE CALLED INTO POLITICS

Regardless how religious, spiritual, sincere or full of prayer he or she is, a person cannot be considered a Christian unless he shows himself to be a good citizen. A part of being a good citizen is being genuinely involved in the political life of nation, state, and community.

The Bible teaches Christian Involvement

There are countless reasons for involvement.

If you read the Bible, you will find God continually involving Himself in the political practices of man. He made a promise to Abraham for kings and nations. To Moses, He gave specific instructions on a political revolution during one of the greatest acts of civil disobedience ever recorded. Moses established a new nation and then led them. At times, they listened and celebrated glorious victories; other times, they did not which led to their defeat.

God spoke regarding justice and righteousness within the political order throughout the prophets. Lastly, when we look at the revelation of God in Jesus Christ, there is a distinct indication: If we claim to be a Christian or follower of Christ, we must involve ourselves in the political processes.

There are some who read the Sermon on the Mount as old-fashioned or an idea that is to be worried about "later" with no relevance to the here and now. But for the people who were able to hear the sermon, they heard an address that correlated to politics and to the current situation in Israel. At that particular time, Israel had been conquered. The Romans had come in and taken away their freedom.

Jesus talked about obeying the laws of the land both in giving obedience to those placed in authority as well as paying the needed taxes. When reading Romans, you see that Paul has written a lengthy piece to address issues that make a good citizen and the requirements: respect for those in authority or in office, the payment of taxes and obedience. Throughout the New Testament, Christians are instructed (encouraged) to obey the law of the land, except for laws that violate religious principles. There is a recurring highlight of honor, respect, and citizenship participation.

Consider law, order, and justice: There can be no justice without the law and order. Likewise, there is no law or order without government. In order to believe in justice, you must believe in political action. Responsible Freedom Calls for Individual Involvement

In all the world there is no one more qualified for political action than a child of God. Our entire faith has pushed to set him on the path with the necessary education he needs to deal with current issues as well as the needs in political action.

History Sets the Pattern

Beneficial change has been opposed by the Church so often just by being linked with the status quo. But through time, over and over the message of Christ, of love in action, has broken through the religiosity to show itself in the lives of men who dared to do differently and get involved, resulting in a developing civilization.

John Calvin's contribution to politics was monumental. He was on the city council and demanded that things be done. Children were falling off of balconies onto streets. He was able to pass a new law requiring a railing to be built onto balconies so that this would no longer be a problem. Also, he instituted a chamber of commerce which would bring employment opportunities to Geneva.

Mary, the queen, had issues with John Knox. He interrupted her court time after time. He insisted that government should be operated for the betterment of the people, not the sovereign. Mary had never heard of such a thing and refused. John Knox finally won Scotland with an evangelical faith and a new idea of government that made Scotland the most productive small nation in the world. All because John was involved with Christian political action.

John Wesley rode through the entirety of England, evangelizing and organizing small groups that developed discipleship and religious instruction. Under his leadership, some social issues of the day were prison reform and the abolition of slavery. His last letter was written to a member of Parliament urging that he vote for the bill to eliminate slavery.

Charles Finney, who traveled the United States, had something to say against racism. Even though he ministered throughout the country, he stated that the reason revival was not coming was because churches were racist. We certainly could use him again.

The Senate was meeting a hundred yards from the Capitol in Washington, D.C. when George Truett stood on the steps and said it would be an immoral act for them not to ratify the League of Nations.

Billy Graham publicly endorsed the Office of Economic Opportunity and the poverty program, stating, "It is a Christian's responsibility to be involved."

In Mississippi, we have actively worked to promote legislation that advances protections for people of faith and lives of the unborn. The Pentecostal church effectively advocated for the passage of the Religious Freedom Restoration Act, as well as, the Freedom of Conscience from Government Discrimination Act. These two pieces of legislation ensure that the state government cannot, in any way, punish people of faith from living out their sincerely held religious beliefs in their every day lives. Additionally, we worked with the Governor and legislators in both chambers to advance pro-life legislation that protects unborn children after a heartbeat is detected. These are just a few examples of what is possible when people of faith take a strong stand in the public square.

These men left us a heritage. Our main purpose of Christian life should be to attack the status quo and dare to be different. We have the Word from God. Now it is up to us. We must embrace the idea of being involved with political action and life. There are endless opportunities and possibilities.

Strategies

First and foremost, we MUST pray. We must never forget the familiar scriptural admonition.

"If my people, which are called by my name, shall humble themselves, and pray, and seek my face, and turn from their wicked ways; then I will hear from heaven, and will forgive their sin, and will heal their land" (2 Chronicles 7:14).

Secondly, political action is somewhat involved with evangelism. "Change the individual, and you change the world" is a cliché which is not totally true but does has some validity. Social order can be changed if individuals will change as well.

Thirdly, the need for education and training is a must.

The Fourth approach operates through the court system. Our nation is built upon law; therefore, many people have gone to the courts for all types of political action.

The fifth operates through legislation – promoting, persuading, speaking with legislators, and accomplishing passage of laws that pertain to our goals.

Whatever you do, while combining spiritual and political, do it in the Name of Jesus Christ.

Read, study, and educate yourself. You will never be an expert on all matters; but if you talk and discuss openly with others, you can learn to be an expert on some things.

Make yourself known in political groups. Vote, get involved, support causes and candidates whom you would like to see in office.

Political Action is **INVOLVEMENT**.

How involved are you?

Chapter Two

PARTICIPATE IN THE PROCESS

Knowing political techniques will help you on your way to becoming an effective citizen. It is vital that the newcomer know the points of access to the political process. In a Democracy, citizens have an open invitation to collaborate and discuss concerns with their political leaders.

The Central Objective

An individual is at the very center of the political process. The entire foundation of our nation understands that one simple man is politically relevant with the welfare of our country being the main purpose of public policy.

We can relate to the political process in many ways. Organizations or an individual make a demand, they become involved in the process. Experts or advisers who are sought out about decisions, become part of the process. Every voter joins in the process. A system is made of each of these moving parts to form the political process.

In *Human Nature in Politics* by James C. Davies, he defines political participation as "taking part in making the basic decisions as to what are the common goals of one's society and as to the best ways to move toward these goals." If there is a belief that their actions are meaningful and lawful, people will invest in politics as long as they are on the receiving end of economic, social, or even intellectual rewards. For some, meeting the "right people" and being involved in a just cause is their reason for being a part of the political system.

New and lifelong friendships are made when we become involved in the political process.

When someone feels strongly about something, be it an issue or a candidate, you will see that spectator become a gladiator.

Leadership in Districts, Sections, or pastors can inspire their members to political participation in various ways. If we can educate often and thoroughly, research shows people will be more likely to participate in politics, and the extent of said participation will be that much stronger. E-mail blasts, church newsletters/bulletins and other published materials can be used to inform and encourage members to vote in both the primary and general elections. In Mississippi, we use CallingPosts the weekend prior to an election to remind pastors to announce the upcoming election on Tuesday. There are occasions when we contact our constituents to let them know about legislation which is being voted on and ask that they call or email their representative.

Group representation by National Apostolic Christian Leadership Conference is a vital part of the democratic process. There is an old proverb that states in "union there is strength". This takes on a very real significance in politics. Our church groups are just now recognizing their potential in this area as they come together for support or opposition.

Another equally important role of National Apostolic Christian Leadership Conference is to notify legislators and our organization when pending legislation will directly affect the Apostolic Movement.

Churches sometimes become very anxious about public policy and may become an interest group themselves or want to speak through the National Apostolic Christian Leadership Conference. Humanitarianism can be a powerful motivator for the churches to become involved with civil rights and welfare legislation.

Chapter Three

Each church/district is perfectly suited to move swiftly and efficiently on a political plane. Churches and Districts have a tailor-made opening for working on social change. No one is better equipped to respond to moral issues facing their city, state, or nation than they are. Not only are they able, but it is also expected that they be intricately invested in the moral climate.

This is mostly given to the fact that a congregation meets regularly, and cooperation is found easily when a group knows and trusts each other. Because they trust and know their fellow members, there is a common duty to honesty, justice and mercy. Even in our current time, the voice of the church has come to be respected within our communities. There is a message of redemption and a solemn responsibility as a stewardship of God's blessings.

The District and local churches are equipped for action on political issues in several ways.

Education

Being a well-versed and educated electorate is key to the success of democracy. Showing a lack of interest in current issues releases others to have their way and encourages disinterest, which in turn defeats the democratic process.

Information

The District through their political Liaison can broadcast information on the current issues and pending legislation to the church in numerous ways. Every possible channel must be used during voter registration or "get out there and vote" push to remind our members of their chance to exercise their civil duty. Some ways to remind people can include a bulletin insert or to include important dates such as General Election day in November onto your church calendars.

Communication

Communications through social media, CallingPosts, email, etc., create an entire new world of responsibility for the church as it faces political issues. These should not be missed as a way to witness to and reach society. No one knows the churches' views outside their doors.

Organization

Organization is a great asset to the district as it encounters politics. If there is an organization they can turn to, the local church will not need to involve themselves in the time and energy it would take to "getting organized".

Action

During World War II, Winston Churchill issued orders to his small staff on notepaper headed with the words, "Action This Day." I present these thoughts that will hopefully lead to actions, the kind of actions that will transform our country beginning at home. Let's look for appropriate ways to make a difference.

Probably one of the most important and neglected pieces of the church's involvement in the political process is Action. It seems the church will discuss and pick apart the question to no end and never act or do anything. We get mad and then we get over it. We sometimes even get everything set up to do something and then stop just short of action because someone was offended or objected.

Two of the best ways churches can get involved and be active is through voter registration and "get-out-and vote" campaigns. No one could argue against making sure your church members are registered to vote or against a reminder to go to the polls. Voting is minimal citizenship.

If these practices are used, no one can say that the "church is telling me how to vote." Those outside of our organization cannot accuse the church of "building a block vote" or of being manipulative.

All that is needed is a solid plan of action for voter registration and get-out-and-vote.

Chapter Four

THE PASTOR AND POLITICS

There is always the question of, "Should a pastor be involved with politics?" The answer: He can never be just an ordinary citizen. His identity as a religious leader is unavoidable no matter how much he might insist that he is acting as an individual. The opportunities available specifically to a pastor come from three different sources:

1. He is most usually seen as a leader in thought and an informed opinion-maker in his community.

2. He is known as a man of convictions, ideals, and religious standards.

3. He is almost solely responsible for the position of one of the most noticeable and viable organizations in society, the church. It would do the pastor well to take a quick look at each of these opportunities.

As Informed Opinion Maker

The very fact that a minister lives in a certain locality and shares the benefits of the community places a degree of civic responsibility upon him. The principal of building rapport and establishing communication within one's community cannot easily be laid aside.

The scriptures provide an interesting commentary on David's success with people:

"All Israel and Judah loved David, because he went out and came in before them."

I Samuel 18:16

Influence is a valuable asset to the ministry.

The duty to keep informed is tremendous. No matter how hard he may try, a pastor cannot get first-hand knowledge.

Issues being debated in the political arena can be quite literally matters of "life or death" for the children of God. Once a matter is discussed and a decision comes forth by the political process, it will affect the lives of thousands, each "made in God's image."

Some of the issues we should care about are:

Abortion	Discrimination
Adoption	Economics
Anti-Semitism	Euthanasia
Business Ethics	Family Law
Censorship	Family Services
Church and State	Foreign Policy
Civil Liberties	Human Relations
Civil Rights	Hunger
Crime	International Relations
Law Enforcement	Religious Liberty

16

Medical Experimentation	Sex Education
Mental Health	Taxes
Planned Parenthood	Vaccinations
Pornography	Violence
Poverty	War - Peace
Prisons and Penology	Welfare Programs
Public Schools	

Pastors have a tremendous obligation as an informed leader in their community to stay informed. Here are some hints for the busy pastor:

As Institutional Leaders

If the church is to be the redeeming force in the world, we must come to the realization that big decisions are made via the political process.

If the church would be the redeeming force in the world, it must come to a new realization that God's love is for all men. A direct result of this is a deep-seated commitment to action in helping people, even if that means to help politically. It is vital for the church to move into the political process.

17

Chapter Five

PREACHING ON POLITICAL ISSUES

Some sermon topics on political issues:

"The Things that are Caesar's"

"Our Church and the National Crisis"

"Law, Order and Justice in Christian Perspective"

"Christian Insights on Civil Disobedience"

"Religious Liberty and Separation of Church and State"

"Christians and the Current Racial Crisis"

"The Menace of Gambling"

"The Things That Make for Peace"

"The Bible Speaks on Taxes and Tax Reform"

"What Shall the Church Do About Pornography?"

"Toward a Christian Interpretation of Sex"

"Blessed Are the Poor"

'Who Are the Poor?"

'Who Is My Neighbor?"

"The Scars of Racism"

This is a task we undertake with both conviction and confidence.

Chapter Six

UNDERSTANDING HOW A CAMPAIGN REALLY WORKS

Deciding About Involvement

    1.   You must determine the need for involvement. It is virtually impossible to link to every issue that is being debated in both the state and local government. This is where it is important to decide whether participation is truly necessary.

Too often, Christians fail to realize the importance for concern with political races. In the past, those of Christian faith were more reactors than initiators in the political process. This means they get involved after the battle has already begun. By that time, points are made, choices are already being formed, and therefore the influence of the church becomes limited between just two men or two positions. Effective action must begin much earlier.

    2. The feasibility of becoming involved. Just as participation needs to be established; there also needs to be discussion as to whether being involved could alter the political outcome. The time, energy and money should not be exhausted on any undertaking that is insignificant or hopeless.

Chapter Seven

HOW A BILL REALLY WORKS

There is a long list of things that should be considered in the making of such a decision. These include:

- Support for the bill.

- Arguments for and against legislation

- Lobbyist groups that would support the bill.

- Lobbyist groups that would oppose the legislation because of vested interests.

- The support or opposition of the Governor, the presiding officers of the House and Senate and key legislators.

- An estimation of the strongest bill that might have a chance of passing.

- An estimation of the weakest bill that could be introduced and still have strength after compromise and deletions.

If the church does not speak up to make their voice heard in the planning of legislation, be it federal, state or local, then they must be happy with what others, who are interested and speaking, decide for them. If districts/liaisons show an interest and speak up, the church could be the driving force behind important legislation that otherwise might not ever be introduced because it does not help or serve the interest of organized best-suited interests.

Introduction of the Bill

There are numerous factors to be considered in the introduction of a bill in a state legislature. Those mentioned before are important; however, of foremost importance is determining the legislative sponsors. When establishing such sponsors, a number of factors should be taken into consideration:

- He/She needs to be a well-known and respected member of their legislative body.

- He/She should be legitimately devoted to the passing of the measure and esteem it so important that they make it a primary matter of interest.

- He/She should have both political and personal connections to those who are initiating the legislation.

- He/She must have the confidence of those who support them.

- He/She must not support or sponsor other legislation that could be or is in conflict.

Also important is the need to determine when the bill should be introduced and in which legislative chambers.

There have been times where churches have made a stand for unimportant legislation. This is a mistake and causes the church to appear, in the eyes of legislation, ignorant and uninformed. When new bills are introduced, we should be sure to carefully evaluate them to determine which ones may truly be of interest. For example, if there is a proposed bill on narcotics, then someone with interest in narcotics should evaluate it using some of these important points:

- Is the man/woman introducing the bill a freshman or an experienced legislator?

- Does the sponsor of the bill show it to be high on his/her priorities?

- Has the measure been introduced before? If yes, how did it fare?

- Was the bill carefully written and prepared?

- On closer look, does it fully represent the best approach to the problem?

-

Committee Assignments

In Mississippi, the Lieutenant Governor appoints Committees and makes assignments.

Current officers in your state have great power. They are allowed to appoint committees, and they are able to choose which committees will handle important legislation. It is customary for such officers to have one or more committees that are a kind of "catch-all." These are usually "State Affairs" or "County, Cities and Towns" and are controlled solely by the presiding officer. In doing this, the presiding officer can send legislation to a favorable or unfavorable committee and receive the support or opposition he is looking for.

The role of the National Apostolic Christian Leadership Conference in supporting or opposing legislation becomes crucial at this point. Because the committee is the first major step in a bill passing, if they find it unfavorable, it will have little chance. Concerned Christians should begin to plead their case and gather information to be sure that the members of the committee are fully and accurately informed. The decisions of the legislator can be influenced by several factors.

- Is this a good legislation for his/her district?

- Is this good legislation for the state?

- Does his/her home district generally favor or oppose such legislation?

- Will the folks back home (particularly financial supporters) be aware of how he/she votes?

- How will his/her vote affect the passage of other legislation?

Legislators often only receive a few well-written letters from the folks back home. These letters describe the feelings as well as show that they are aware of his/her votes. They may also receive a phone call from a pastor or another community leader to sway a man's vote. This is easy to do if a legislator does not already have a strong opinion on a particular subject. He/she may not have facts or be aware of arguments for your position.

One of the main reasons for a phone call could simply be an effective way to show your legislator that someone is closely watching his/her vote. It is most important to remember that those who communicate with their legislators must have accurate facts. Your legislator normally makes decisions based on the research and facts he/she is given; therefore, he relies on others to be accurate in their representations.

The Rules Committee

This committee is responsible for setting measures for floor debate.

Chapter Eight

WORTHWHILE RELATIONS WITH AN ELECTED OFFICIAL

The same practices and approaches that work well in human relations usually work well in the political arena. There are two basic factors that make up politics: people and principles. Effective political communication involves an accurate understanding of people and a sound presentation of principles.

Public officials are just like any other human. They love to succeed but hate to fail; they trust their friends and are guarded around strangers. They respond to approval and react to mistreatment. Just like you, they are irritable when sick or tired and enjoyable to be around when they are feeling well. There is a respect for truth and resentfulness towards deceit. They experience all the same day-to-day problems we do while making a home, earning a living, being a parent, performing business or professional duties, meeting social, civic, and church commitments – plus the passed down problems of a large wide-ranging constituency.

As many know, public officials do not live in a vacuum. From the moment they reveal their desire in public office, they are subjected to scrutiny, publicity, criticism, idolatry, ostracism and being tantalized.

Many of them are extraordinarily educated and lead with a greater array of knowledge and a much broader awareness of issues, conditions, and viewpoints than in the past. Most of them are educated, somewhat sophisticated, and skilled administrators.

Experience has trained them to be both practical and realistic in order to excel in politics: to gain favor and nomination of a political party, to guide a campaign, to convince a majority of voters favorably, and to succeed daily in the political arena, a highly competitive profession.

Most public officials are allies of Christians:

"For rulers are not a terror to good works, but to the evil. Wilt thou then not be afraid of the power? do that which is good, and thou shalt have praise of the same."

Romans 13:3

How, then, do we go about opening the channels of communication so that ally would unite with ally – friend to relate to friend?

There is a firm foundation for National Apostolic Christian Leadership Conference or district political Liaison to act on the idea that the legislator wants to make the right decision and make a creditable stand. This helps to have a shared objective in which they can progress to a point where they are in complete agreement, therefore achieving unity in purpose.

The Relationship

One of THE most important things to remember is that a public official needs a genuine friend. A friend who shows interest in them and respects them as a person as well as the office which they hold. We as

Christians, can fill a vital need in a public official's life: you can be a friend!

You might have been friends before his/her entry into public life or even the one who encouraged them to see public office. Perhaps your first meeting could have been when you took the time to attend a reception, coffee or rally during the political campaign. These pre-election relationships are significant for future contacts. Your friendship and support are most remembered when received before victory is guaranteed. This becomes the basis of a mutual confidence and alliance.

A significant relationship can be developed and nurtured even after election. In the beginning, the motives of such a relationship will probably be questioned by the official. Early on in public office he/she will be made aware of fair-weather relationships and their fragility and how they can quickly fade off.

Worthwhile relationships are started and enriched by paying attention to activities such as:

1. Invitations to receptions and coffees honoring candidates are often open to the public, and attendance gives encouragement to the candidate. Take time to attend. This is an informal opportunity to make contact and show evidence of your personal interest, encouragement, and support.

2. Ask for your name to be placed on the official's email list for any material or information he/she may send out. Make sure you show interest in a few specific areas or issues that his/her office has connected with.

This simple request is a reminder to the official of your involvement and impact you have on his/her work.

3. Make contact with the official once in a while for information or an opinion on something you may need. This shows that you have confidence in them as well as the import you place on his/her work.

4. Take notice of his/her associates and reach out to them, become acquainted with their environment. Those closest to him/her will be of great assistance to you in making contact with the official when matters of urgency arise.

5. From time to time, your District Board meetings may require a special speaker. Invite your public officials to fill one of these engagements. They appreciate any opportunity to meet their constituents during positive situations and share topics of public concern. This also helps to ensure that everyone gets to know their legislators too.

6. At some point in time, your legislator is going to have a specific need, be it encouragement, counsel, campaign work or financial support. All you need to do is be willing to be a helpful Christian friend when that need arises.

The Objective

We do not govern ourselves directly in our republican form of government. Our laws are made, clarified, and implemented through elected officials. It is imperative that our views and beliefs are expressed skillfully so that we have a voice in how we are governed.

The purpose of political involvement is to offer guidance to governmental processes corresponding to the United Pentecostal Church viewpoints and beliefs by using honest, productive reasoning and influence.

From the very beginning of childhood, we each learn ways of getting what we want. Add to those useful suggestions for use in the political world to achieve success:

1. Realize that you must allow for different opinions. Your opinion is just one of many that your legislator must hear. There must be compromise on his or her part for a working solution. Remember, compromise is not always an indication for weakness or even failure; but rather represents a marked maturity and progress.

2. There is always power in sound reasoning, logical argument and reliable facts. An official can think one way, but using those traits, you give them an opportunity to change their minds. There is always an opportunity to influence; done correctly, you have the power to sway.

3. The only true way to lose is to give up. Do not fall into prejudgment or be overconfident. You can jump to the conclusion, let up and see yourself in the exact opposite end result that you thought might happen; win or lose.

4. It may become needful for an official to make a decision or vote in a way that does not

accurately represent their true position so that a larger, more important goal is achieved. Do not judge them from the viewpoint of one decision. They face, sometimes daily, very trying conflicts between their own personal convictions and the demands of those whom they serve.

5. Someone may fight against you on one issue, but on another stand persistently with you and fight with you on important matters. There's an old saying that it never hurts to have too many friends. The best practice is to not burn any bridges within the political arena. This results in the fire starter being burned more than anyone else and the loss of a potential ally at a later date.

6. Throughout this entire process, keep sight of your goal. Never lose your reason for your struggle. Sometimes you will have to celebrate the partial success. Take that success, reassess, and plan on the best way to achieve the remaining goals.

The Issue

The winner of the political arena will not always be the good ideas or honorable causes. It takes someone who is honorable and trustworthy to make those ideas and causes their own personal concern, then to take action.

The political arena is inundated with other ideas. Ideas that are powerfully motivated by self-interest, substantial self-centeredness for personal advancement and large economic factors. All in competition with each other and truly great and honorable proposals.

You can help your causes by giving them ways to advance using some basic guidelines.

1. Your issue will most likely be something that will be attractive to the human nature of many public figures. Use this to promote and gain their support. This will advance the official's public image and he/she will not be able to ignore it. Make this your point.

2. Educate yourself! Knowing your facts and being well educated on subjects will ensure that your official will feel it is well worth his/her time to talk with and listen to you. Be sure that when doing your research, you notice where your argument is both weak and strong. Understand there may be some validity to the opposing argument.

3. Once you know your issue, be sure to research your official. Find out what his/her past opinion was on the subject. If you are unsure, take the time to ask them and discuss it with genuine desire and not just as a way of argument. When you do so, you have a fuller understanding on how to word and work for your issue.

4. Choose wisely! Be sure to choose just one or two issues instead of multiple. When you try to champion too many at a time, your issues could become an obstacle that most will turn a

blind eye to, and the real issues can go unnoticed.

5. If you want to help your official, be sure that your issue is well researched, represented well, and engaging. Assume that he/she has none and give them all they need. He/she does not always have the time or facts, but if you have done your work, they can focus on the actual issue with understanding and therefore advocate.

The Contact

Communication is key! Everything you have read and prepared for comes down to this. If you are silent in your support, your support is meaningless. Idle influence equals no influence.

We cannot believe that if we don't see a reason to speak up, our elected officials will do it for us. It amounts to neglect and failure on our part if we choose to stay silent.

Once we have reached out and fostered a friendship, have a clear and concise goal in hand and educated ourselves, we are able to make an impact. At that appointed time, make contact and communicate!

1. Make personal contact. When you make that personal visit, it indicates that you have made this a high priority. This gives you power above the normal words and argument, but more importantly, the power of your personality and sincerity. You get to establish a dialogue, have questions answered, alleviate

doubts, neutralize vacillating and answers to be evaluated.

You can show your official that you appreciate the value of his/her time as well as the significance of the matter of importance, when you make an appointment to meet without interruptions. Try meeting in a neutral place, such as meeting over a meal in a quiet place. This also gives your meeting a more casual feel so that they are at ease.

2. Sometimes it is not feasible to have a face-to-face meeting. It's ok to make telephone contact. This can still be a very personal reach out. Be sure that it is very clear as to who you are and the reason for your call.

3. One of the oldest ways of contact can still work. Written contact does lack a lot of the effect and personal influence, but with thought and a well-placed word, it can be just as valuable.

There are some do's and don'ts when it comes to political communication:

DO:

- Be sure that the communication is yours and yours alone.

- Show the official that you have complete confidence that he will make the right decision.

- Be sure to give personal experiences supporting your belief.

- Lean on practical experience to demonstrate your viewpoints.

- Be clear, convincing and concise.

- Check your facts and use only reliable data.

- Appreciate when you are trusted with confidential information.

- Use discretion when exercising your influence.

DON'T:

- Use a template.

- Resort to insult, mistreat or threaten.

- Beat around the bush, be vague or dull.

- Presume that your views are known or that the official knows where you stand and why.

One of the most important things to worry about is timing. In the Political world, there is a constant ebb and flow, sometimes very significantly so. Both inside and outside conditions have major roles in deciding political futures. You will know when the time is right. When you see the moment, do not hesitate. Act quickly. Oftentimes, if you wait until you see or hear something in the news, you have waited too long.

There is no time for procrastination. Be willing to act quickly on short notice while the issue is at hand. Using both action and effort combined, you can achieve effective communication.

It seems that in today's time, gratitude has become a neglected custom. There is always time and need for expressions of appreciation. In Mississippi, there has been success sponsoring friendly recognition receptions such as the Legislative Prayer Breakfast.

Written on the front of the National Archives in Washington, D.C., is this admonition:

Eternal vigilance is the price of liberty.

Liberty is a personal advantage. Eternal vigilance becomes a personal responsibility. You cannot truly live as a Christian in this world and see the need for Christian concern and influence and still say, "It is nothing to me."

Chapter Nine

WHAT IS A POLITICAL LIAISON?

Political Director/ Liaison Job Description
Principal Responsibilities

In coordination with the National Political Director, advance the organization's mission and issue priorities through a comprehensive strategy that links issue advocacy to grassroots base-building at both the grassroots/state and national levels.

Support the process of setting overall goals and timelines for legislative priorities which have been set by the National Apostolic Christian Leadership Conference and the local district board.

Develop and manage strategic relationships with other faith organizations in your district to help advance the National Apostolic Christian Leadership Conference legislative goals on the State and National Levels.

Provide the means for grassroots assistance to community-based organizations on a range of priorities, including, but not limited to, religious liberty, pro-life, pro-family and pro-liberty advocacy.

Frequent travel throughout the district to work with local partner churches to raise funds, meet with pastors, labor and local and statewide political leaders.

Represent the district and the National Apostolic Christian Leadership Conference in speaking engagements, and update the National Political

Director, Staff on the progress/status of initiative in the state.

Work with other member church staff and pastors to build their understanding of the issues being advocated for by the National Apostolic Christian Leadership Conference and the district. Provide them with tools and strategies in the context of faith community organizing.

Qualifications

Experience in community outreach and political work including the ability to communicate with the superintendent, board members and pastors, and managing implementation of legislative strategies for significant statewide and local legislative campaigns.

Strong background in and understanding of community organizing with a demonstrated ability to relate to legislators and other faith/community organizations and volunteer grassroots members and leaders.

Strong commitment and passion to building the political power/influence of the church, toward achieving the vision established by the National Apostolic Christian Leadership Conference, the district and the United Pentecostal Church.

Strong knowledge of and experience with national, state and local political players engaged in the public square.

Strong understanding of the legislative process and how to manage a legislative campaign.

Demonstrate leadership ability.

Strong teambuilding, facilitation and coalition-building skills.

Excellent oral communication, public speaking and writing skills.

Experience and comfort working in a multi-disciplinary and multi-cultural environment.

Strong understanding of legal parameters for electoral organizing in both 501(c)(3), 501(c)(4) and PAC contexts preferred but not required.

This position reports to:

Local District Superintendent and the National

Political Liaison for the National Apostolic Christian Leadership Conference.

QUOTABLE QUOTES

Our lives begin to end the day we become silent about things that matter.

-Martin Luther King, Jr.

When the eagles are silent, the parrots begin to jabber.

-Winston Churchill

The Constitution is not an instrument for government to restrain the people; it is an instrument for the people to restrain the government—lest it come to dominate our lives and interests.

-Patrick Henry

Knowledge is proud that he has learned so much; wisdom is humble that he knows no more.

-William Cowper

The federal government must and shall quit this business of relief. To dole out relief is to administer a narcotic, a subtle destroyer of the human spirit.

-Franklin Roosevelt

Opinion is a flirting thing,

But Truth, outlasts the Sun;

If then we cannot own them both,

Possess the oldest one.

-Emily Dickinson

"...Render therefore unto Caesar the things which be Caesar's, and unto God the things which be God's."

-Jesus - Luke 20:25

MAKING HISTORY

"The most important thing is to **bring people to Christ;** - the **second most important thing** is to **preserve the freedom** to do **the most important thing!"**

Rev. John Witherspoon (1723-1974) was a Scottish Presbyterian pastor and President of Princeton who was a delegate to the Continental Congress where he signed the Declaration of Independence.

Rev. John Peter Muhlenberg (1746-1807) was a Lutheran pastor in Virginia who became a major general during the Revolutionary War, a U.S. Congressman and a U.S. Senator.

Rev. Frederick Augustus Muhlenberg (1750-1801) was a Lutheran pastor in New York who was elected a U.S. Congressman and was the First Speaker of the House, signing the Bill of Rights.

Rev. Abiel Foster (1735-1806) served as pastor in Canterbury, New Hampshire, a delegate to the Continental Congress, the New Hampshire Legislature and a U.S. Congressman.

Rev. Benjamin Contee (1755-1815) was an Episcopal pastor in Maryland who served as an officer in the Revolutionary War, a delegate to the Confederation Congress, and a U.S. Congressman.

Rev. Abraham Baldwin (1754-1807) served as a minister at Yale, a chaplain in the Revolutionary War, a delegate from Georgia to the Continental Congress, a U.S. Congressman and a U.S. Senator. He is the founding president of the University of Georgia.

Rev. Paine Wingate (1739-1838) was a pastor in Hampton Falls, New Hampshire, who served as a delegate to the Continental Congress, a U.S. Congressman and a U.S. Senator.

Rev. Joseph Montgomery (1733-1794) was a Presbyterian pastor in New Castle, Delaware. Married to a sister of Dr. Benjamin Rush, he served as a chaplain in the Revolutionary War with Colonel Smallwood's Maryland Regiment.

He was elected a delegate from Pennsylvania to the Continental Congress, a judge and a representative in the State Assembly.

Rev. James Manning (1738-1791) was a Baptist pastor in Rhode Island who was the first President of Brown University where, during the Revolutionary War, he allowed General Rochambeau's French troops to camp on the campus grounds. He was elected a delegate to Congress.

John Joachim Zubly (1724-1781) who was a Presbyterian pastor in Georgia who was a delegate to the Continental Congress.

Signer of the Constitution **Hugh Williamson**, born December 5, 1735, was a licensed Presbyterian preacher.

When Evangelist **George Whitefield** began preaching the **Great Awakening Revival** in **Philadelphia** in 1739, he inspired the idea that the **city** should have **a school for blacks and poor orphan children.**

ABOUT THE AUTHOR

David D. Tipton was elected in April 2009 and continues to serve as the Superintendent for the Mississippi District United Pentecostal Church International. In addition, he serves as the General Board representative to the Building the Bridge ministry of the United Pentecostal Church, Executive Board member of Tupelo Children's Mansion, Board Member of New Beginnings Adoption Agency in Tupelo, Mississippi, Executive Board member of Stand Up 4 Mississippi, and member of the Mississippi Governor's Council on Teen Pregnancy. Previously, he served as Executive Director of Promotions for North American Missions Division at World Evangelism Center in St. Louis, Missouri for two years.

Prior to accepting the position as Promotions Director in 2007, he served in various ministerial capacities. For ten years, he was the Director of the North American Missions Division of the Mississippi District and pastor of The Pentecostals of Grenada, Mississippi. His first pastorate was of the First Pentecostal Church in Georgetown, Louisiana. During his time in Louisiana, he served as Assistant Pastor of the First Pentecostal Church of Leesville, Louisiana and served as Section six youth director.

Reverend Tipton was born in Port St. Joe, Florida. He and his wife, Gwen, have four children: sons Devonn, Damon, and Matthew and daughter, Rachael. They have ten grandchildren.

Products by David Tipton

Mississippi Matters
Perspective & Insights from David Tipton
A compilation of articles written to the great people
of the Mississippi District United Pentecostal Church

Gonna Tell Everybody
CD by David & Gwen Tipton
Produced by Kenny Henson

Faith, Freedom & Politics
A guide for a Christian in civic life
Available Soon

Adam Had No Childhood
Shared Experiences & Short Stories

Contact Information:
Onward365
David Tipton
P. O. Box 1852
Grenada, MS 38901

**If you would like more information on
how to become a partner with National
Apostolic Christian Leadership
Conference (NACLC), go to
www.naclc.org.**

Made in the USA
Middletown, DE
02 September 2024

60228743R00035